BOOK 2

David Carr Glover

MW01055165

FAVORITE SOLOS

14 OF HIS ORIGINAL PIANO SOLOS

Each year Alfred publishes a variety of sheet music solos for students at various levels. Teachers and students use them for recitals, auditions, festivals, or just to have fun. Many of these become student favorites, and teachers continue to teach them through the years. When Alfred purchased Warner Brothers Publications in 2005, the sheet solos of David Carr Glover (1925–1988) became a part of the Alfred catalog.

The piano-teaching world is seldom gifted with a composer who can write music that is at once artistic and pedagogical—David Carr Glover was one of these rare talents. Glover's well-crafted pieces are motivating and exciting, while demonstrating an awareness of students' technical and musical abilities at each level.

Alfred is pleased to introduce *David Carr Glover's Favorite Solos,* book 2, a collection of 14 late elementary to early intermediate solos for students of all ages. Students, teachers, and audiences alike will enjoy the variety of styles, sounds, and moods of this music. The pieces included in this collection have maintained their popularity among pianists throughout the years, and will quickly become your favorites, too. Enjoy!

CONTENTS

Alfred Music Publishing Co., Inc.
P.O. Box 10003
Van Nuys, CA 91410-0003
alfred.com

ISBN-10: 0-7390-6544-0
ISBN-13: 978-0-7390-6544-0

Flags on Parade

David Carr Glover

Snappy march time

Sneaky Creepy Things

David Carr Glover

Not too fast, and sneaky

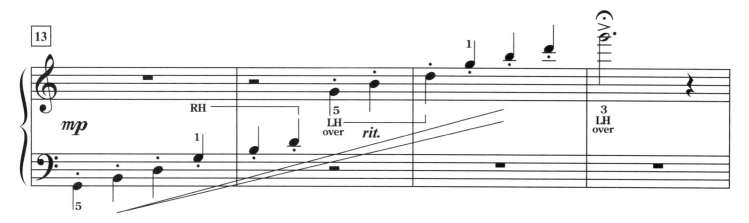

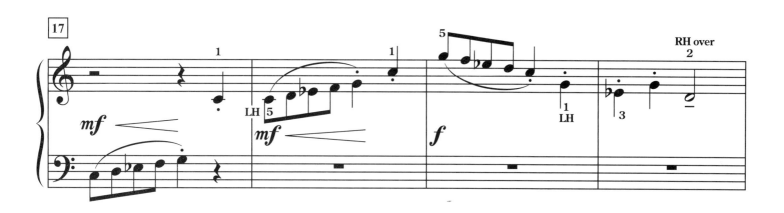

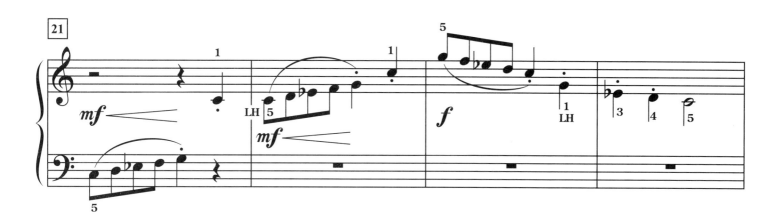

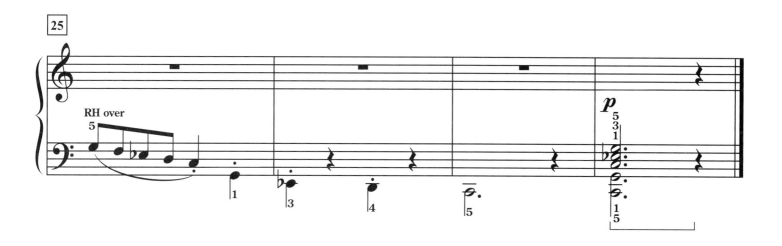

Drifting

David Carr Glover

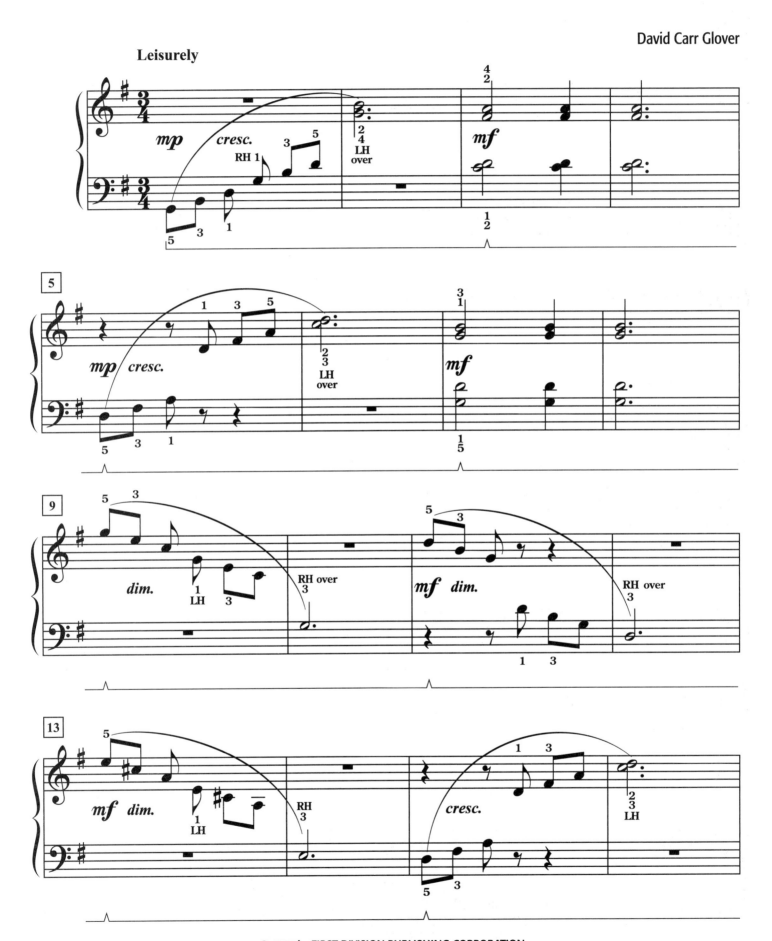

Japanese Garden

David Carr Glover

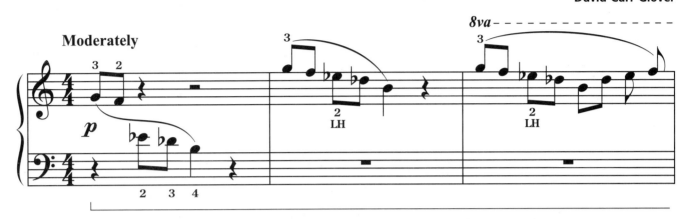
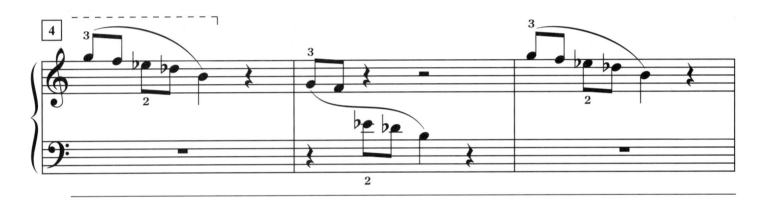

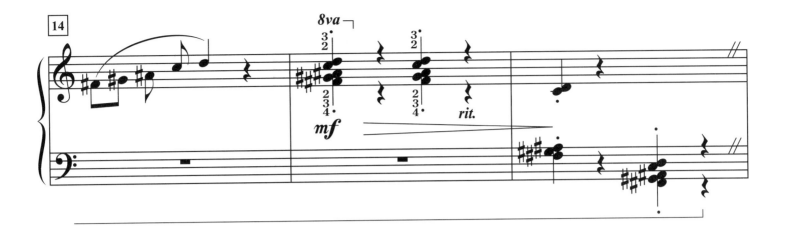

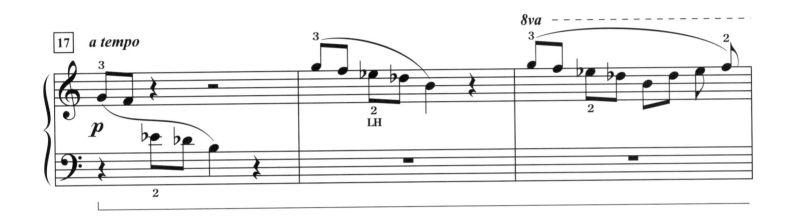

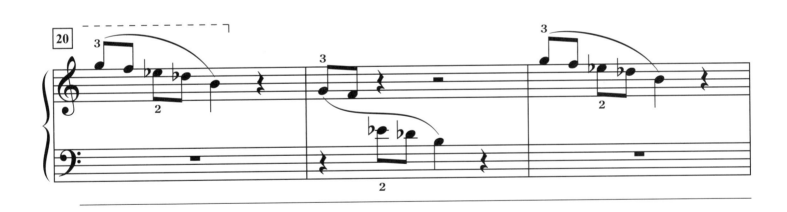

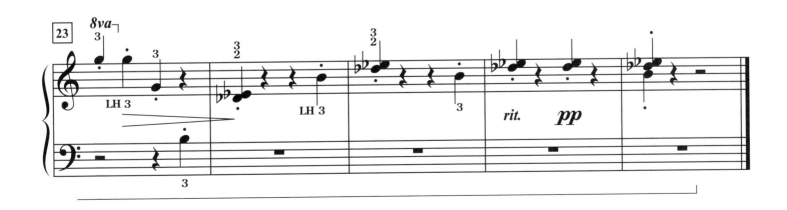

Our School Band

David Carr Glover

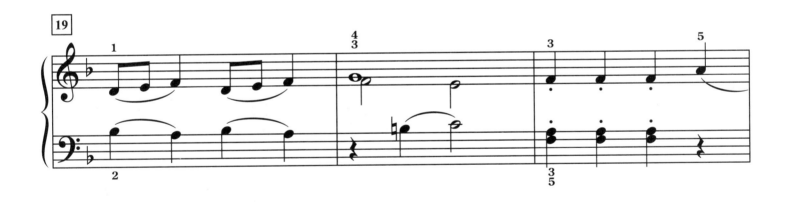

to John Martin

The Great Cathedral

David Carr Glover

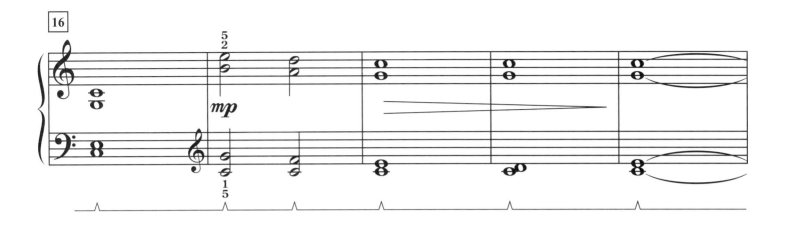

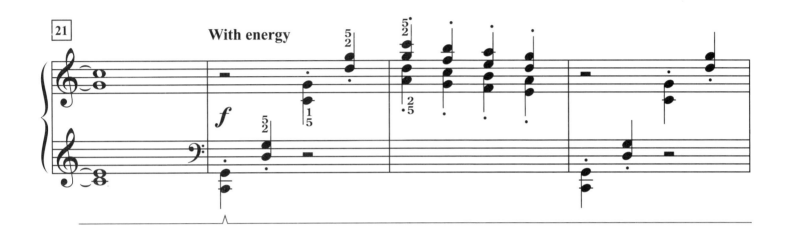

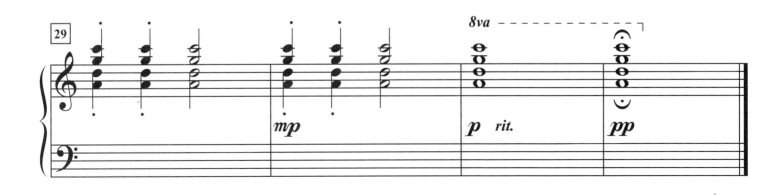

Spooky Games

David Carr Glover

15

Soular Bear

David Carr Glover

March of the Fleas

David Carr Glover

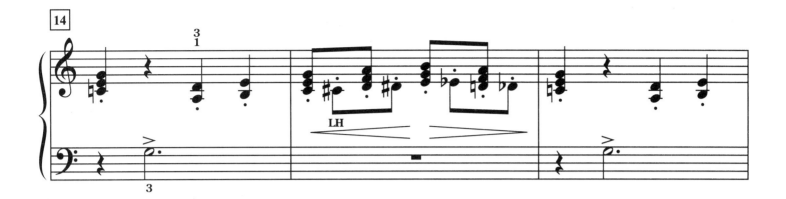

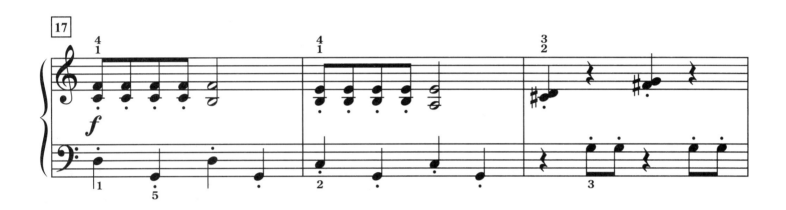

Evening Concerto No. 1

David Carr Glover

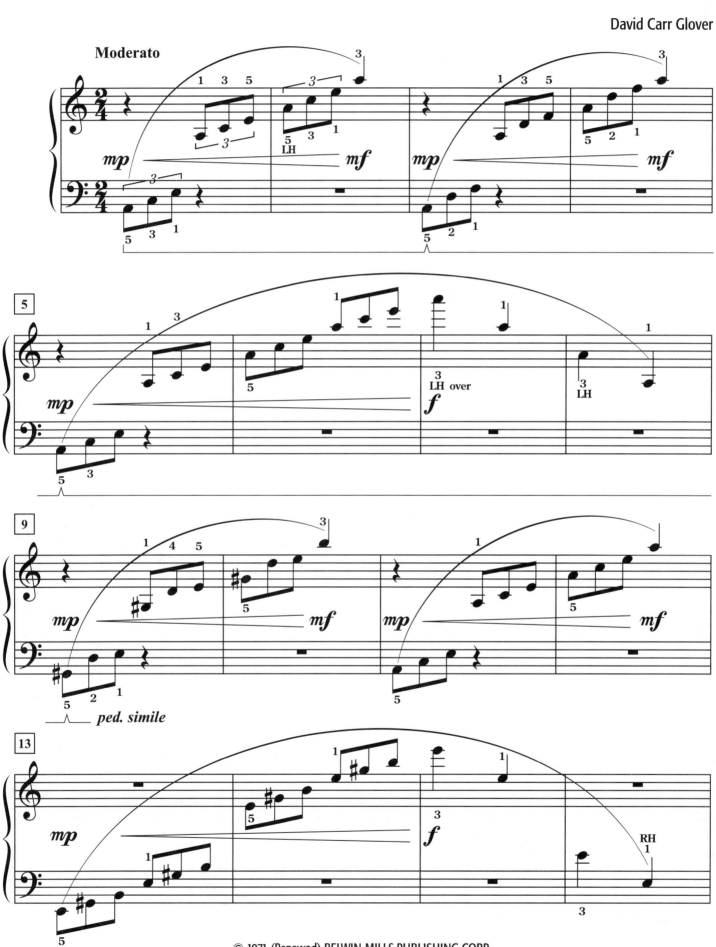

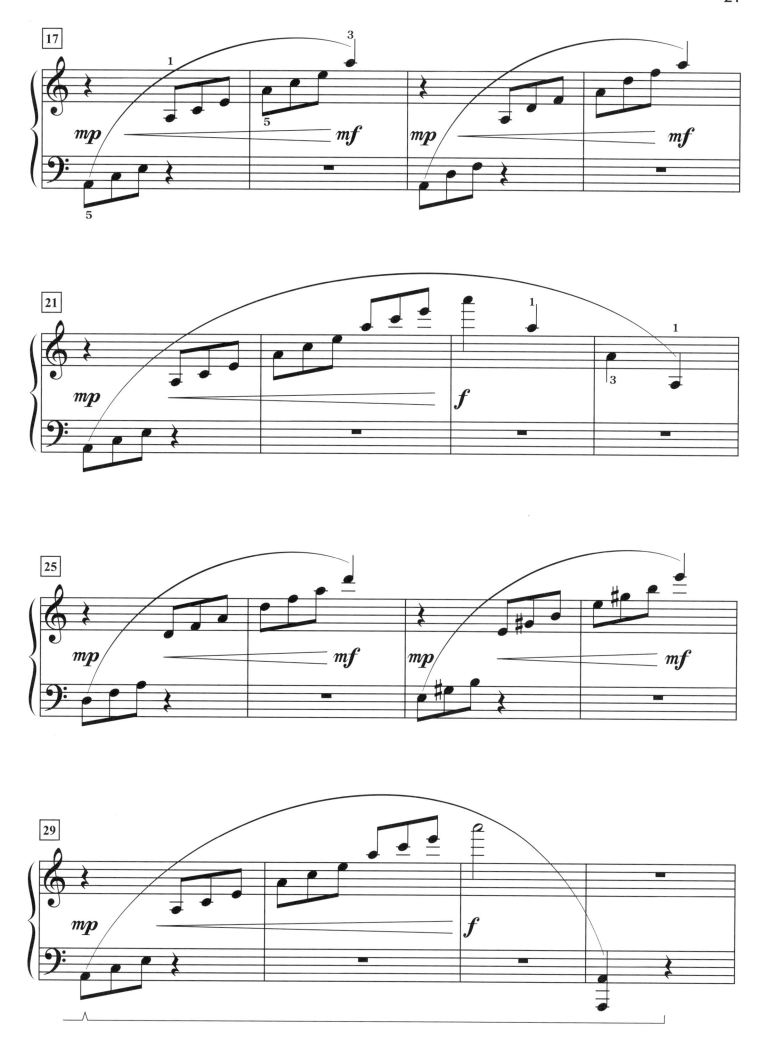

22

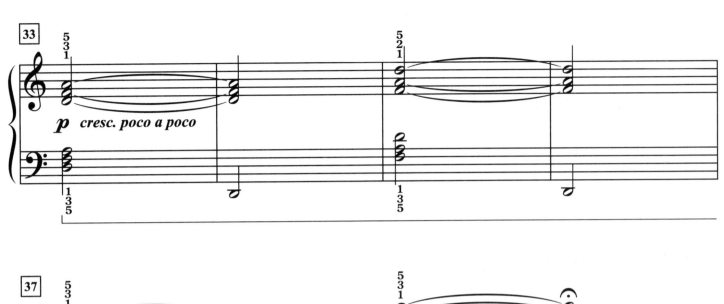

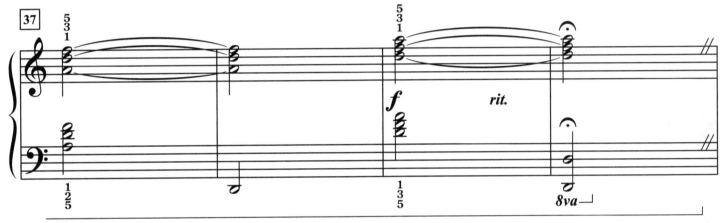

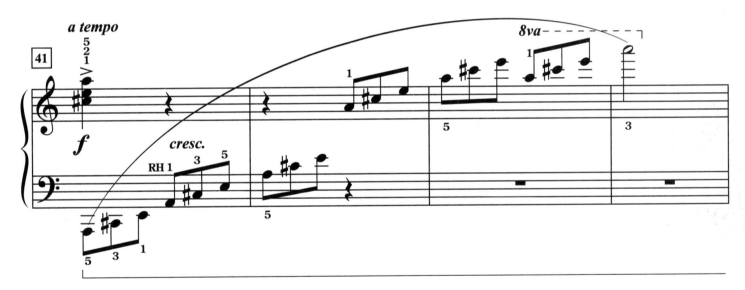

to Judy Vogan

Moon Mist

David Carr Glover

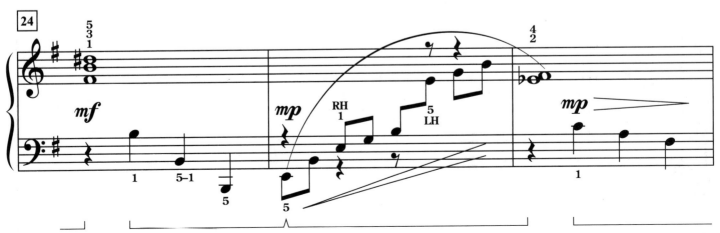

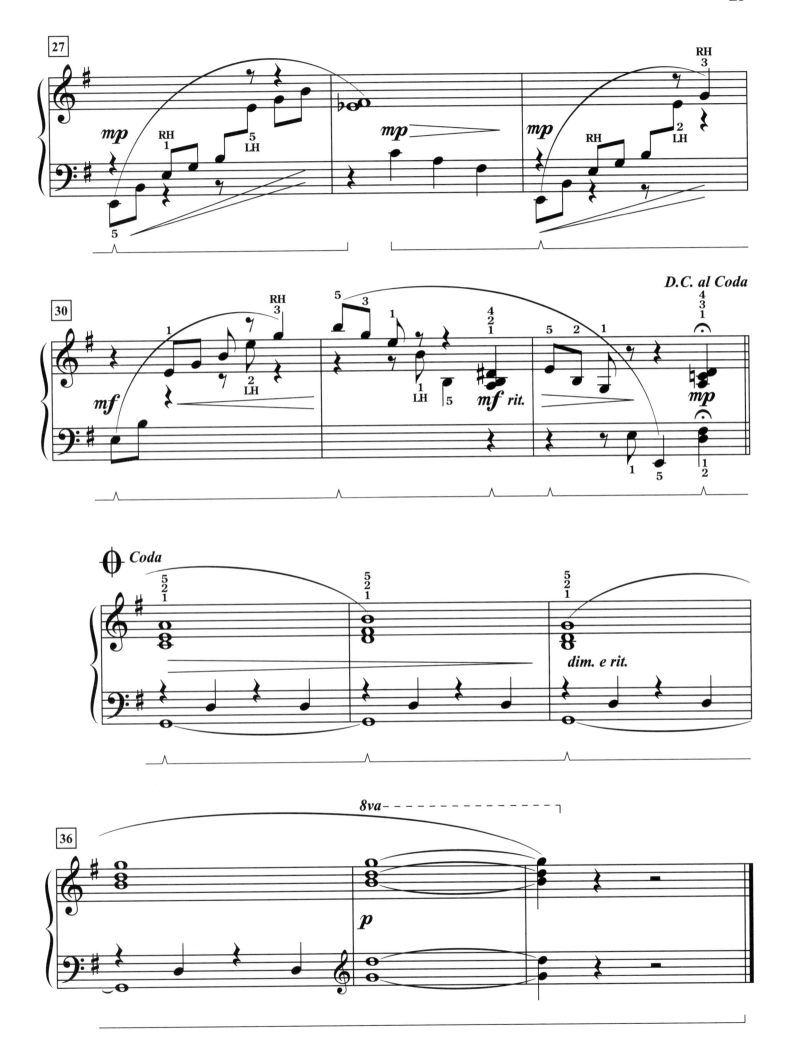

to Isabel and Charles Hansen

Candlelight Supper Club

David Carr Glover

Guitars

David Carr Glover

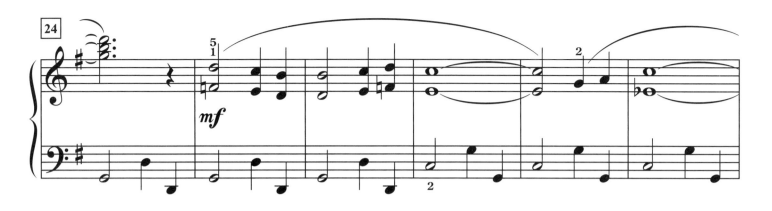

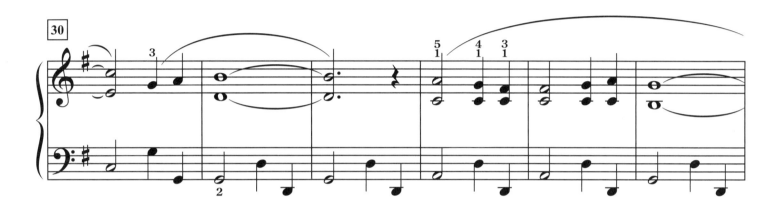

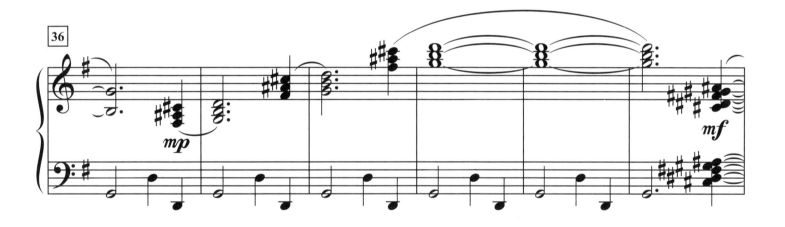

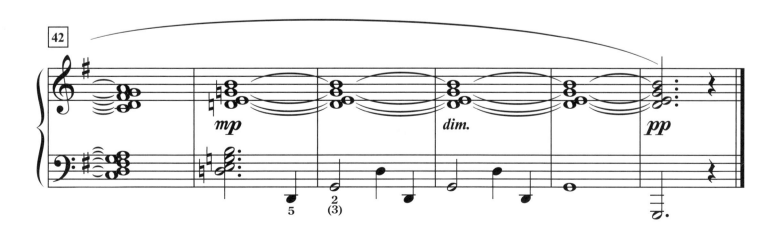

Hoe Down

David Carr Glover

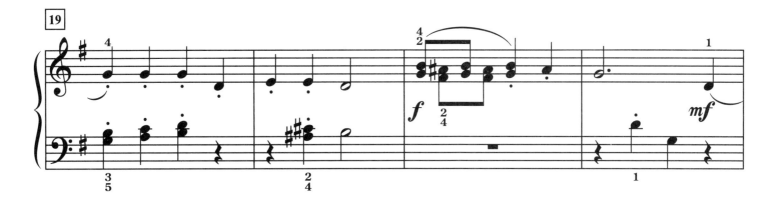

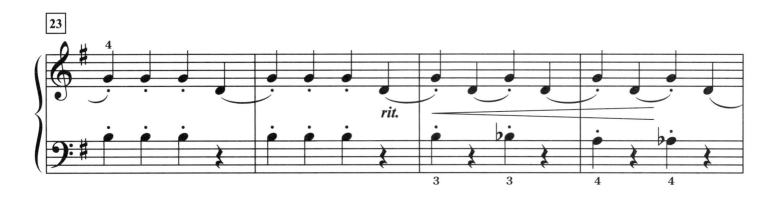

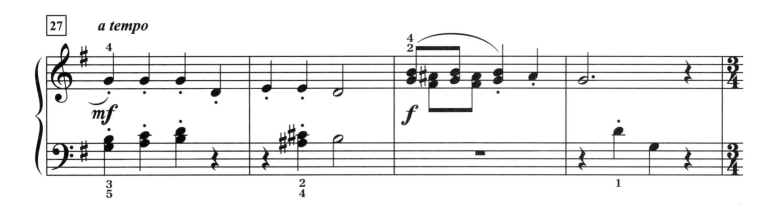

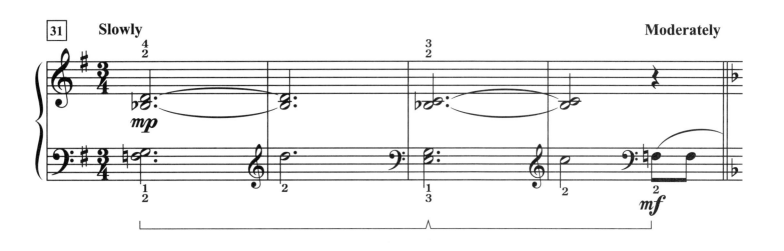